THAT'S LIFE
PictureStories

BOOK 6
Caring

Tana Reiff

LAKE EDUCATION
Belmont, California

Cover Design: Ina McInnis
Text Designer: Diann Abbott

Library of Congress Catalog Number: 94-079122

ISBN 1-56103-781-8

Printed in the United States of America

1 9 8 7 6 5 4 3 2 1

The Marcianos

■ Frank Marciano *He owns a grocery store and has something to say on every subject.*

■ Marge Marciano *She listens to everyone's problems and knows how to help.*

■ Ernesto Marciano *Frank's father retires from life until he meets Rosa Esteban.*

■ Gina Marciano *The Marcianos' daughter is very much her own woman.*

■ Doug Kelly *He and Gina Marciano have a life plan that works for them.*

The Adamses

■ Walter Adams *Keeping up with a growing family has its problems.*

■ Ruth Adams *She manages to keep her cool through all of life's surprises.*

■ Pat Adams *A 13-year-old learns something new about life every day.*

■ Tyrone Adams *At 16, does "Mr. Basketball" really know it all?*

The Estebans

■ Carlos Esteban *Since his wife's death, he's both father and mother to his children.*

■ Rosa Esteban *Carlos's mother doesn't let age stand in the way of happiness.*

■ Rick Esteban *He finds that it's easy to get in trouble when you're 16.*

■ Roberto Esteban *This 14-year-old boy is making big plans for his future.*

■ Bonita Esteban *Growing up means having to learn about all sides of life.*

The Nguyens

■ Nguyen Lan *She can handle being a single parent in a new country.*

■ Nguyen Tam *At 4, he asks his mother why he has no father at home.*

Rosa Esteban gets a lot of mail

Don Kaufman is delivering mail on his route. His last stop is at the Estebans'. Kaufman tells us that Mrs. Rosa Esteban sends away for a lot of booklets. She gets free booklets on many different subjects from the government. Rosa says that learning new things keeps her young.

How does Kaufman know so much about Rosa?

Rosa is on the run

Rosa comes running into Frank and Marge Marciano's food store. She is in a hurry.

"I need a dessert to take to the ROC meeting," Rosa says to Frank. She had forgotten to bake something.

Marge asks what "ROC" means. Rosa tells her that it stands for Rights for Older Citizens.

Then Marge shows Rosa a cheesecake.

"Fine," Rosa says. So Marge rings up the sale.

What is one "right" an older person might want?

Ernesto has other plans

Frank's father, Ernesto, comes into the store.

"Hey, Pop," calls Frank. "Are you going to the meeting with Mrs. Esteban?"

"No, Frank," says Ernesto. He wants to go back to the basement and work on his wood carvings.

But Frank has other ideas. He wants his father to go out and have fun.

"I *am* having fun," Ernesto says. "I don't need to be around a lot of people to have fun."

What kind of person do you think Ernesto is?

Ernesto gets talked into it

"Ernesto, you have good health," says Rosa. "You should go out more. We have a good time together, don't we?"

"Sure," Ernesto answers. "I like being with *you.*"

Frank tells Ernesto that if he doesn't get out of that basement, he'll turn into a mushroom. But Ernesto likes working on his wood carvings. Then Rosa takes Ernesto by the arm.

"Today," Rosa says, "you have to come with me."

Do you think Ernesto should listen to the others?

The SOS bus is free

"Go with Rosa, Pop," adds Marge. "The break will do you good."

Rosa says that the meeting today is about income tax.

"Now *that* sounds like fun," laughs Frank.

"Do we have to ride that bus with the big SOS on the side?" asks Ernesto. "SOS" means Senior Overland Service. But sometimes those letters stand for a call for help—Save Our Ship. That's why the SOS makes Ernesto think that the bus will sink.

Do you think that special buses for older people are a good idea?

Don't wait up!

Rosa hears the bus coming. She runs out the door with Ernesto walking behind her.

"Don't wait up!" Ernesto calls to Frank and Marge.

"They're a cute couple," Marge says to Frank. Frank isn't so sure that he agrees.

"I love Pop," Frank says, "but he sure can be difficult to live with."

"That's something that seems to run in the family, Frank," Marge says with a wink.

What does Marge mean when she says, "That's something that seems to run in the family"?

A walk in the park

Ernesto and Rosa are walking home from the meeting. Ernesto notices that Rosa's face looks a little red.

Rosa says that she is fine, but she wants to sit down. Ernesto sits down with her.

"I'm really very glad to be alive on a day like this," Ernesto says. "I like being with you."

Rosa feels the same way. Her son Carlos and his children make her very happy.

"But when I'm with you," Rosa says to Ernesto, "it fills an empty spot for me."

What person in your life makes you feel glad to be alive?

Love is something special

Ernesto loves his family, too, but he doesn't always show it. He says that even with family, everyone needs someone his or her own age. Ernesto is trying to tell Rosa that he loves her. But Rosa has known this for a long time.

"But," she says, "we can't afford to get married."

Do you hide your feelings sometimes?

Rosa thinks of her family

Ernesto gets a pension. He thinks they will have enough to live on if they put their incomes together.

Ernesto has $2,479 in savings. Rosa has $4,000 from her husband's life insurance. That money can help if their income is not always enough.

"But who would take care of my grandchildren?" Rosa asks.

"You can still visit them when they need you," says Ernesto.

Do you think that Rosa should think of herself or her grandchildren first?

I do

Ernesto knows that Rosa loves her family. But she needs time alone, too. Rosa thinks that he means she should spend time away from him! But he wants the two of them to be alone together.

"Will you marry me?" Ernesto asks.

Rosa finally says yes. She will talk to her son, Carlos. And Ernesto can tell Frank and Marge.

Do you think that everyone needs time alone?

It's almost too exciting!

Rosa wants to take the bus home. Suddenly she doesn't feel very well. It might be the heat. It might be the idea of marrying Ernesto. It might be a little bit of both.

"Is it all right if we wait?" Rosa asks.

"For the bus, forever," says Ernesto. "For you, I don't want to wait another day!"

How do you feel after you have made a big decision?

Frank can't believe it

Frank explodes when he hears the news.

"GET MARRIED?" Frank screams. Frank thinks that Ernesto is too old. And he thinks that his father doesn't have enough money to get married. Marge thinks that the news is wonderful.

"Marge, are you crazy?" Frank asks her. "Did you hear him?"

"Frank, *you're* the one who isn't listening," says Marge. Frank is doing all the talking.

Why do you think Marge likes the idea of Ernesto marrying Rosa?

Where will the money come from?

"Pop, what would you live on?" Frank asks his father.

Ernesto tells him what he and Rosa had talked about on the bus ride home. He says that they know how to be careful with money. Frank wants to know how he will be able to pay his doctor's bills.

"I can take care of myself!" Ernesto says.

Could Rosa and Ernesto afford to live in your town?

Ernesto's mind is made up

Frank is angry. He thinks his father is being foolish. He tries to tell Ernesto what to do.

But Ernesto has made up his mind. He doesn't need his son to tell him what to do. Ernesto leaves. He slams the door on his way out.

How are Frank and Ernesto alike?

Carlos is taken by surprise

At the Estebans' apartment, Rosa breaks the news to her son Carlos. Carlos doesn't seem very happy about it.

"Don't you want me to be happy with Ernesto?" Rosa asks. "I've always wanted *you* to be happy."

Carlos wants his mother to be happy. But it's hard for him to think of his mother as someone's wife. He forgot that she was both wife and mother before. She knows how to be both.

Why might Carlos not want his mother to get married?

A life of her own

Carlos feels as if one of his kids were leaving home. But Rosa is not one of the kids. Carlos will grow older, too.

"When you're alone like me," says Rosa, "I hope you'll find someone you love, too."

Carlos knows that his mother is right. He knows that she has a life of her own. He wants her to be happy. He is ready now to tell the kids that Rosa is getting married.

How do you think Rosa's grandchildren will take the news?

Good news travels fast

Bonita comes rushing into the room.

"The kids heard!" Bonita calls happily. Bonita and her brother Roberto were in the kitchen. They were doing their homework when they heard Carlos and their grandmother talking.

"The door was open just a little," says Roberto. "We could hear everything."

Do you think that Rosa is sorry the children have heard the news?

The kids give Rosa the OK

The children are happy that their grandmother is getting married. They like Ernesto, too. Besides, they are old enough to take care of themselves. Roberto has a friend who plays in a band. Roberto would like the band to play at the wedding.

"I want to be the best girl," says Bonita, "or whatever it's called."

How do you think Bonita and Roberto make Rosa feel?

The uninvited guest

There is a knock on the door, and Frank rushes in.

"Carlos!" Frank yells. "Did you hear what these two old . . ." Then he sees Rosa. He doesn't finish his sentence.

"Do you go for this?" Frank asks Carlos. Carlos says that he doesn't see why they shouldn't get married. That makes Frank feel as if no one sees things his way.

Why do you think Frank comes to see Carlos?

Everyone loves a wedding

Kaufman loves weddings because they are such happy times. He says that things will work out fine for Mrs. Esteban and Mr. Marciano. They knew each other for a long time before they decided to get married. Frank isn't too happy about it—but everyone else is. Rosa and Ernesto's wedding is going to be soon.

_____

How do weddings make you feel?

Rosa asks about Frank

Rosa and Ernesto are sitting together in the park.

"Has Frank calmed down yet?" Rosa asks Ernesto.

"He still thinks that we're too old," says Ernesto. "He thinks that we can't make it on our own. But he'll see!"

Rosa tells Ernesto that he has a beautiful smile. He smiles because he is happy.

Do you think that a person can be too old to get married?

Rosa has plans for Ernesto

Rosa is glad that Ernesto is happy. She has news for him. She has put his name down to help out at the Senior Citizens Center. She wants him to deliver meals to people who can't get out.

"I can't do that," Ernesto says. "Older people make me sad."

Why do you think Rosa didn't ask Ernesto before she signed him up?

Rosa has more plans

Rosa is sure that Ernesto will help at the Center. She wants him to do something else, too. She wants him to be a grandparent to a child who doesn't have one.

"I can't do that, either," says Ernesto. "Kids make me nervous."

Rosa really wants him to help. She says that everyone needs help some time in life.

When was the last time you helped someone?

Ernesto says no

Rosa reminds Ernesto that people help him. For one thing, he pays only half the bus fare. He can go to ball games for half-price. He can do this because he is a senior citizen.

"Well, I still don't want to deliver meals or take care of kids," says Ernesto.

Why do you think senior citizens need help from others?

There's time enough

Ernesto is ready to leave the park. But Rosa wants to sit for a while longer. She still feels tired.

Ernesto's life with Rosa is just beginning. So he makes a special toast to bring good luck.

"To this moment and to the moments that follow," Ernesto says to Rosa.

Suppose you are beginning something new and exciting.
What could you say for a special good-luck toast?

Something is wrong

Carlos, Bonita, and Roberto are at the hospital. Carlos is very nervous.

"I just saw Rick and Mr. Marciano out front," Roberto tells Carlos. But Carlos isn't really listening. He is worrying about his mother, Rosa.

What do you think is wrong?

Ernesto is very upset

Rick and Ernesto rush into the hospital. Ernesto is very upset. He wants to know what has happened to Rosa.

"They think that she had a stroke," says Carlos.

The news is too much for Ernesto. He starts speaking in Italian. Carlos helps him sit down. They should be hearing from the doctor soon.

Why do you think that Ernesto starts speaking in Italian?

The doctor breaks the news

Finally the doctor comes into the hall.

"I'm sorry, Mr. Esteban," the doctor says. "There was nothing that we could do. It was a massive stroke. She was gone before . . ."

"I understand," says Carlos softly. "Thank you."

"*Per piacere,*" cries Ernesto in Italian. "*Madre mia!* Oh, please . . ."

Ernesto prays for a favor (*per piacere*) in Italian.
What favor do you think he is praying for?

Kaufman knows what to do

Kaufman is standing outside a flower shop. He thought that the flower shop would be fixing wedding flowers. Instead, they're fixing the family's funeral flowers for Rosa. Carlos has asked people to give to charity in Rosa's name. They could do that instead of sending flowers.

"I'm going to give to charity," says Kaufman. "And I'll still send a note . . . something short and simple. For a writer, I seem lost for words right now."

Would you rather send flowers or give the money to a charity?

Marge helps out

Marge stops by Carlos's apartment. She has brought the family some dinner. She knows that he has a lot on his mind. He probably doesn't feel like cooking.

"Thanks, Marge," says Carlos. "How's Mr. Marciano doing?"

"He's very upset, of course," says Marge. "But we think he'll be all right."

Do you think that Carlos is glad to see Marge?

Planning ahead

Carlos says that Rosa's death was a surprise. The family wasn't ready. But you can never be ready for something like that.

Marge tells him about Harold Marouski. He belongs to a memorial society. The group helped Harold plan ahead for his own funeral. Alice, Harold's wife, says that it's been good for the family.

Do you think Carlos is interested in what Marge is saying?

Rosa wanted a simple funeral

Harold Marouski wants to be cremated, not buried. Planning ahead will help the family know what to do. They will save money on the funeral, too.

"It's important to save money these days," says Carlos. "Mama always said she wanted a simple funeral. But there's no such thing these days."

What does Carlos mean by "a simple funeral"?

What is best?

I feel awful worrying about the money. She gave us so much. I shouldn't shortcut her funeral.

Why don't you just make it simple, as Rosa wished? After all, it's her funeral.

You're right, Marge.

Carlos feels awful to be worrying about the money. He wants his mother to have the best. So he thinks that he should pay whatever it costs to have a big funeral. But Marge has other ideas.

"Why don't you try to keep it simple?" Marge says. "That's the way Rosa wanted it. After all, it's her funeral."

Carlos has to agree.

Do you think that Carlos should do what Rosa wanted or what he wants?

Carlos makes a decision

This has made me think about when I die. I want to plan my own funeral. I don't want my kids to have to go through this.

Maybe Alice and Harold can come over to talk to Frank and me. They can help us plan everything.

I want to come, too.

Carlos has a lot of decisions to make about Rosa's funeral. It has made him think about what he wants when he dies. He decides to plan his funeral ahead of time. He doesn't want his kids to have to do this.

Marge is thinking the same thing. She would like to ask Alice and Harold Marouski over. They could tell Frank, Carlos, and her about funeral planning.

Why do you think that planning a funeral ahead of time might be a good idea?

Frank will have the last laugh

"I can already see the words on my gravestone," laughs Marge. "'Here lies Marge . . . wife of Frank Marciano. Rest in peace . . . *at last*!'"

"Frank will love that," Carlos says. Then Carlos begins to laugh along with Marge.

"I know Frank," says Marge. "He would probably laugh, too!"

Do you think that Marge has made Carlos feel better?

Nobody likes funerals

Marge and Frank are driving to Rosa Esteban's funeral. Frank hates to go to funerals.

"Nobody likes them, Frank," Marge says. "But Rosa was our friend. We just have to go."

"People stand around trying not to look at the body," says Frank. "Talking about nothing."

Marge has to tell Frank how to drive. He is too busy talking.

What should a person say to the family of someone who has died?

There wasn't much to say

Frank doesn't want people looking at him when he's dead.

"Maybe no one will even come to your funeral, Frank," jokes Marge. "Watch, the light's turning!" She sees that Frank isn't watching the road.

"Have you talked to your father about Rosa dying?" asks Marge. Frank told his father that he was sorry, but that was all. Frank and his father never talk about things like this.

Why do you think Ernesto walked away when Frank tried to talk to him?

For better or worse

Marge tells Frank where the funeral home is. But he knows where it is. He turns right at the next corner.

"Hey, I mean it," Frank says. "I don't want people looking at me when I'm dead. I want our friends to remember me just as I am now."

"For better or worse, right?" jokes Marge.

Do you think that Marge will remember Frank's wishes when he dies?

Kaufman will miss Rosa

"Mrs. Esteban was buried today," Kaufman says. Everyone will really miss her. There was a big crowd at the funeral. Then friends and neighbors took food over to the Estebans'.

"A death in the family does one thing," Kaufman says. "It pulls us all together."

How does a funeral bring people together?

Rosa helped many people

Carlos thanks Mrs. Weinberg for all her help.

"Well, Carlos," says Mrs. Weinberg, "your mother was a wonderful woman. She helped so many of us. There's no way to pay that back."

Mrs. Weinberg had worked with Rosa at the Senior Citizens Center. The Center has five services, and Rosa worked in all of them. The Center helps about 165 people. And Rosa knew most of them.

What do you think Mrs. Weinberg will remember most about Rosa?

The good things are easy to remember

Mrs. Weinberg says that Rosa did a lot of good work. One week the two of them had 46 shut-ins to take care of. These people needed meals delivered to them. Rosa always worked very hard and never complained.

It makes Carlos feel good to hear this.

Why does Mrs. Weinberg tell Carlos these things about Rosa?

Frank and Marge try to help

Marge is helping Carlos take care of things. She sends Bonita Esteban to her friend's house. Then she looks for Frank. Frank has gone into the kitchen. He wants to get a cup of coffee for his father.

But Frank can't find Ernesto. He heads outside, but he stops to talk to Carlos on the way.

"Listen, Carlos," Frank says. "If there's anything I can do—well, you know."

"I know," says Carlos. "Thanks."

What is something that Frank could do for Carlos?

Frank talks with his father

Frank finds his father outside.

"Where are you going?" Frank asks.

"Oh, Frank," Ernesto answers, "I was going to the park where Rosa and I used to walk."

Frank walks along with Ernesto. He wants to talk to him.

"I'm really sorry about Mrs. Esteban," Frank begins. "It doesn't seem like 20 years ago that Mom died, does it?"

Ernesto agrees. It doesn't seem that long ago.

What makes Frank remember his mother just now?

Ernesto makes plans

Ernesto remembers how Rosa wanted him to be a grandparent to a child who doesn't have one. He decides to do it. Frank is sure that Rosa would like that.

Frank is sorry that he was against his father marrying Rosa. He tries to tell his father.

"I know," says Ernesto. "You're hard-headed, but you get it from your family. From your mother's side, that is."

Is it always easy for a parent and a grown child to have a heart-to-heart talk?

The last is best

Frank jokes with his father to make him feel better. Then he tells him the Robert Browning poem that Don Kaufman wrote down:

> Grow old along with me!
> The best is yet to be,
> The last of life, for which the first was made.

Frank asks if the last part of life is the best. Ernesto smiles.

"At times like this, Frank," Ernesto says, "it's the best."

Do you think that this story has a happy ending?